The Library of Living and Working in Colonial Times™

A Day in the Life of a Colonial Sailmaker

Laurie Krebs

The Rosen Publishing Group's
PowerKids Press™
New York

For my friend, Elise Broach
With thanks to Gary Adair and Karl Steinmayer, Mystic Seaport, Connecticut, and to Matt Baldwin,
UK Sailmakers, Norwalk, Connecticut

Published in 2004 by The Rosen Publishing Group, Inc.
29 East 21st Street, New York, NY 10010

Copyright © 2004 by The Rosen Publishing Group, Inc.

All rights reserved. No part of this book may be reproduced in any form without permission in writing from the publisher, except by a reviewer.

First Edition

Editor: Frances E. Ruffin
Book Design: Emily Muschinske

Photo Credits Cover (right), title page (right), p. 4 (right) © The Historical Society of Pennsylvania/*James Forten*, Artist Unknown, c. 1800-30, American Negro Historical Society Papers, Gift of Leon Gardiner; cover (left), title page (left), pp. 4 (inset), 16 Science, Industry, and Business Library, The New York Public Library, Astor, Lenox, and Tilden Foundations; pp. 7, 8 (inset) © North Wind Picture Archives; p. 8 Independence National Historical Park; p. 11 © SuperStock; p. 12 © Hulton/Archive/Getty Images; p. 15 © Mystic Seaport, Mystic, Connecticut; p. 19 © The Mariners' Museum, Newport News, Virginia; p. 20 © Nancy Carter/North Wind Picture Archives.

Krebs, Laurie
A day in the life of a colonial sailmaker / by Laurie Krebs.— 1st ed. p. cm. — (Library of living and working in colonial times)
Summary: Describes a typical day in the life of James Forten, who was born in Philadelphia to free black parents, learned to be a sailmaker, and later became a wealthy, respected businessman with his own shop.
Includes bibliographical references and index.
ISBN: 978-1-4358-3686-0
1. Forten, James, 1766–1842—Juvenile literature. 2. African Americans—Biography—Juvenile literature. 3. Sailmakers—Pennsylvania—Philadelphia—Biography—Juvenile literature. 4. Free African Americans—Pennsylvania—Philadelphia—Biography—Juvenile literature. 5. African American abolitionists—Biography—Juvenile literature. [1. Forten, James, 1766–1842. 2. African Americans—Biography. 3. Sailmakers—Pennsylvania—Philadelphia—Biography. 4. African American abolitionists—Biography. 5. Pennsylvania—History—Colonial period, ca. 1600–1775. 6. United States—History—Colonial period, ca. 1600–1775.] I. Title. II. Series.
E185.97.F717 K74 2003
623.8'62—dc21

2002000100

Manufactured in the United States of America

James Forten was a sailmaker and a wealthy businessman who lived in Philadelphia. Although the descriptions of Mr. Forten's day-to-day responsibilities are fictionalized, the events of his life and the details about sailmaking in colonial times as described in this book are true.

Contents

1	James Forten, Sailmaker	5
2	The Sail Loft	6
3	Growing Up in Philadelphia	9
4	The War Years	10
5	A Game of Marbles	13
6	From Apprentice to Owner	14
7	Just for Good Measure	17
8	Rows and Rows of Stitches	18
9	Eyelets, Cringles, and Roping	21
10	James Forten, Citizen	22
	Glossary	23
	Index	24
	Primary Sources	24
	Web Sites	24

James Forten, Sailmaker

James Forten walked down Pine Street to the docks on Philadelphia's **waterfront**, where sailing ships were anchored. On this summer morning in 1798, hundreds of white sails **billowed** in the morning breeze. At the sight of them, James's heart swelled with pride. He mounted the stairs to Robert Bridges's sail **loft** where he had worked for many years as a sailmaker. The shop now belonged to James. Philadelphia, Pennsylvania, was an important colonial seaport. Experienced sailmakers were always needed. James was one of the best.

◀ *James Forten made sails like those on this sailing ship (inset). A free black man, he was proud of his skills and of his business.*

The Sail Loft

As a boy, James visited his father where he worked, at Bridges's loft. James remembered the needles and knives, the balls of twine, the sharpening tools, and the lumps of beeswax tucked in place at one end of the sailmaker's bench. He would put on his father's leather palm, which looked like a leather glove, and pretend he was pushing needles through thick layers of cloth. Today James looked at the huge, wooden loft floor, as smooth as glass. His sailmakers would not get splinters as they sewed while sitting on this clean floor.

This is a drawing of a sailmaker's loft in the 1880s. The tools and methods of making sails were unchanged for many years. ▶

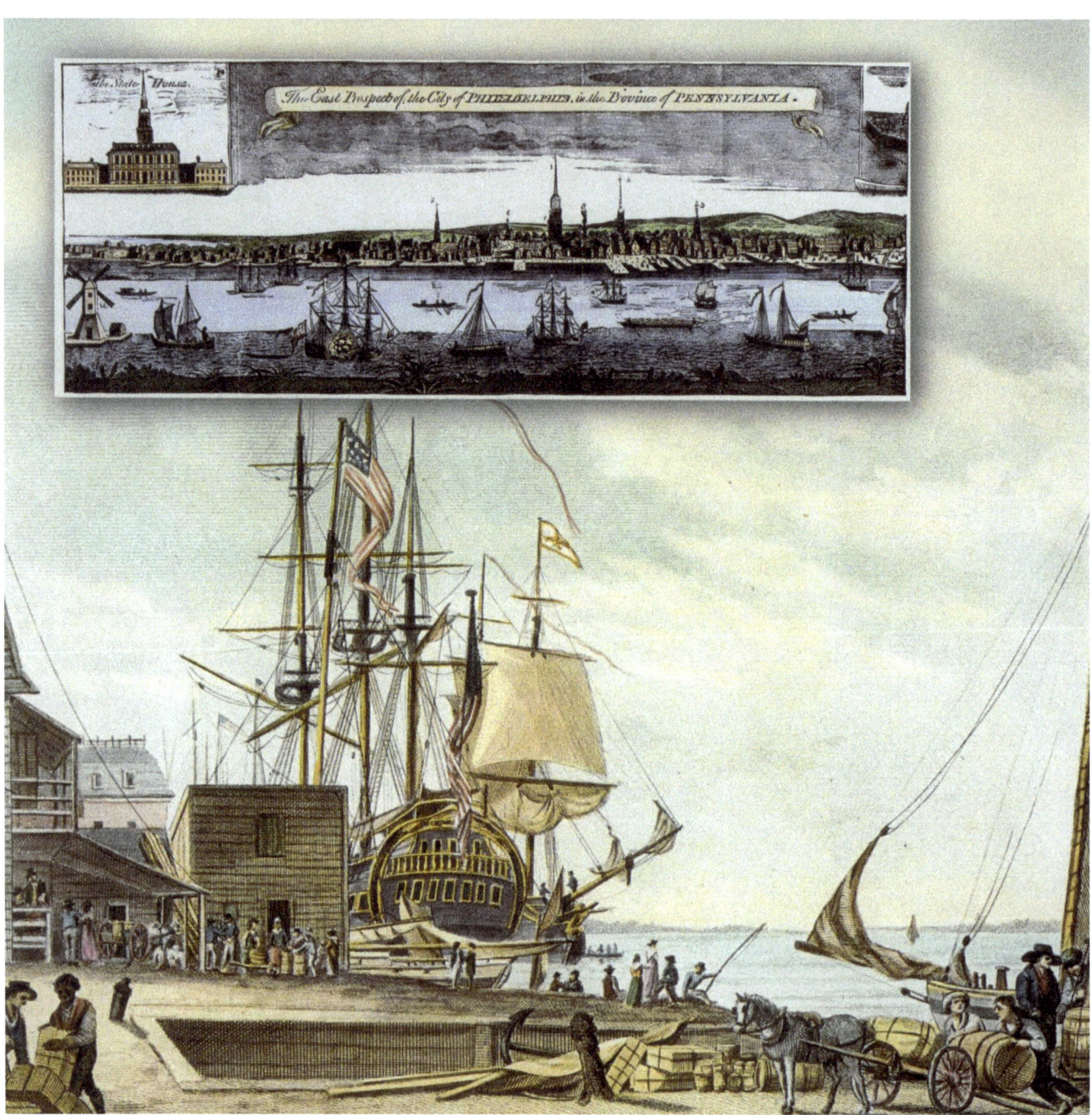

Growing Up in Philadelphia

Born in Philadelphia in 1766, James Forten was the son of free black parents. Many black people at that time were slaves, especially those who lived in southern colonies. James's family lived next to the docks, near the shop where his father worked. James loved to climb aboard the tall sailing ships. He loved to watch the **canvas** sails billow in the breeze. James attended a **Quaker** school where he learned to read and write. When he was nine, his father died in a boating accident. James left school to go to work.

◀ *This is a scene of Philadelphia's waterfront and the Arch Street ferry. Inset: Philadelphia in 1751, as seen from the Jersey shore.*

The War Years

For several years, James worked in a grocery store. He was too young to work in the sail loft. In 1781, when he was 15, the colonies were fighting against Great Britain in the **American Revolution**. James signed up as a powder boy on an American ship, the *Royal Louis*. He carried gunpowder from below the ship's deck up to where the cannons were fired. The *Royal Louis* won its first two battles against the British navy but lost the next one. James was among those captured and taken prisoner aboard the British ship *Amphyon*.

The Bonhomme Richard, *commanded by Captain John Paul Jones, defeated the British ship* Serapis *in 1779.* ▶

A Game of Marbles

Although James was a free person in Philadelphia, British officers sent black prisoners to the **West Indies** and sold them into slavery. James was frightened when he saw the captain looking at him. The captain was really looking at the leather pouch of marbles James held. He took James to meet his son. For several days the two boys played marbles and became friends. Instead of being sent to the West Indies, James was kept prisoner on a British ship, the *Jersey*. A bag of marbles saved him from a life of slavery.

◀ *During the American Revolution, as many as 11,000 prisoners died on British prison ships such as the one in this picture.*

From Apprentice to Owner

This morning, as his sailmakers arrived for work, James remembered the day in 1784 when he became an **apprentice** to Mr. Bridges. It was unusual to have black and white men working together, but Robert Bridges judged his sailmakers by their skill, not by the color of their skin. James was bright and hardworking. When James was 20 years old in 1786, Mr. Bridges made him **foreman** of the loft. Most of the sailmakers liked working for James. Mr. Bridges sold his shop to James when he retired in 1798.

This 1918–1920 photo shows men in a Maine sail loft making sails in the same way that sails had been made for centuries. ▶

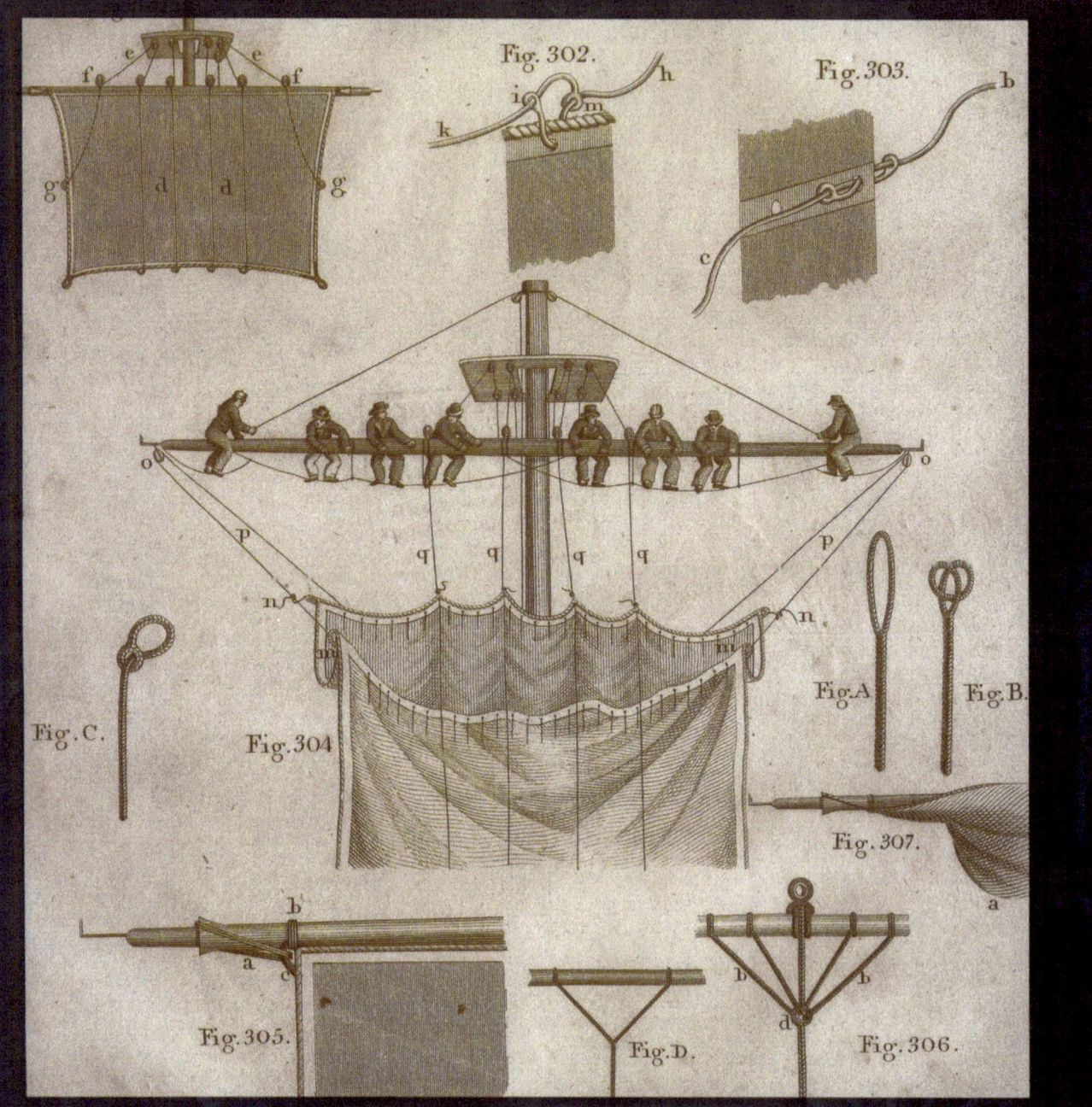

Just for Good Measure

James checked the measurements on a new set of square sails for a ship anchored at the waterfront. Last week, he and an apprentice had climbed up the ship's **rigging** to the **yardarm**, where the sails were to hang. They measured across the top, the bottom, and the sides. This ship would have six square sails for each **mast**. Measuring was an important job. Sails had to fit perfectly. The bottom of each sail had to be curved so it would not chafe, or rub, against the frame in the wind. Extra canvas was needed for seams and hems.

◀ *This 1819 picture shows how sails were made and attached to the rigging.*

Rows and Rows of Stitches

Meanwhile, James's workers were cutting canvas for the sails of a different ship. Canvas came in different widths. The sailmakers laid long strips of it side by side on the loft floor to match the width of the sail's pattern. They sewed the pieces together with two rows of stitches. They marked the sail's measurements on the cloth. Only then did James allow them to cut out the shape of the sail. Deep hems called tables were folded and sewn in the top and the sides of the sail. A special hem was made for the curved bottom.

This is an eighteenth-century sailmaker. For added strength, several layers of cloth were stitched to the corners of a sail. ▶

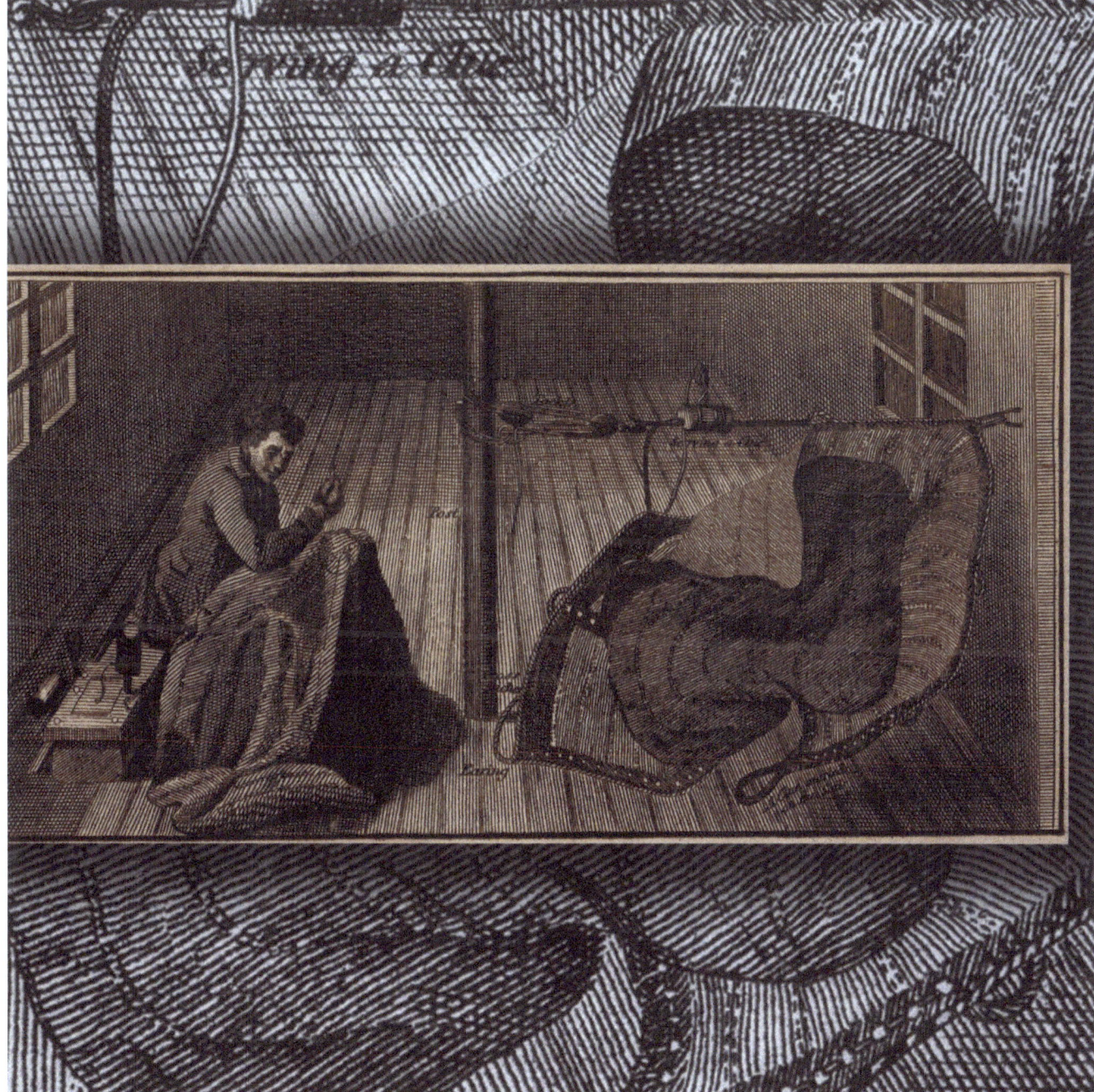

Eyelets, Cringles, and Roping

Across the room, an apprentice punched a row of holes in the top edge of James's sail. He sewed eyelets, or loops of twisted rope shaped like tiny doughnuts, into the holes. The many eyelets fastened a sail to the ship's yardarm. Cringles, or holes that were much larger than eyelets, had metal rings inside the loops. They were placed in the corners of a sail so that ropes could be attached to hold the sail tight. Finally, a long piece of rope was stitched around the edges of the sail to frame and protect it. At last the sail was finished.

◀ *Stitching rope around the edges of a sail protects it from hitting the rigging and tearing the canvas during a storm at sea.*

James Forten, Citizen

James Forten was a good citizen, a good husband, and a good father to his eight children. He was one of Philadelphia's richest businessmen, respected and honored by his community. Much of his energy and wealth was spent trying to improve the lives of black Americans. He worked to end slavery. He used his home as a hiding place for escaped slaves and paid for the freedom of others. Late in the day, James said good night to his workers. As had Mr. Bridges, he judged them by their skill, not by the color of their skin.

Glossary

American Revolution (uh-MER-uh-ken reh-vuh-LOO-shun) Battles that soldiers from American colonies fought against England.

apprentice (uh-PREN-tis) An inexperienced person who is learning a skill or trade.

billowed (BIH-lohd) Swelled out with the wind.

canvas (KAN-ves) A strong cloth with a coarse weave, often made of cotton.

foreman (FOR-min) A worker who is specially trained or in charge of others.

loft (LAHFT) An upper floor of a warehouse or business building.

mast (MAST) A long pole that rises from the deck of a ship, and that holds rigging and sails.

Quaker (KWAY-kur) A person who practices a religion that believes in peace and in equality for all people.

rigging (RIG-ing) Lines and chains that support a ship's sails.

waterfront (WAH-ter-frunt) A section of a town that lies along a body of water.

West Indies (WEST IN-deez) The chain of islands lying between the United States and South America.

yardarm (YARD-arm) A wooden pole that supports the head, or top, of a sail.

Index

A
American Revolution, 10
Amphyon, 10

B
Bridges, Robert, 5, 9, 14, 22

C
canvas, 17–18

F
foreman, 14

H
hem(s), 17–18

J
Jersey, 13

L
leather palm, 6

P
Philadelphia, Pennsylvania, 5, 9, 13, 22

S
sailing ships, 5, 9
sail loft, 5–6, 10
slavery, 13, 22
slaves, 9, 22

W
waterfront, 5, 17
West Indies, 13

Y
yardarm, 17, 21

Primary Sources

Cover, page 4. *Portrait of James Forten*. Watercolor, artist unknown (c.1800–1830). From The Historical Society of Pennsylvania, from the American Negro Historical Society Papers. **Cover, page 4 (inset).** *Engraving of a ship from The Young Sea Officer's Sheet Anchor*. Darcy Lever. (1819). From the Science, Industry and Business division of the New York Public Library. **Page 7.** *A sail loft in Maine*. Woodcut by J. MacDonald (1885). Published in *Harper's Weekly*. **Page 8.** *Arch Street Ferry, Philadelphia, Pennsylvania*. Engraving by William Birch & Son (1800). From Independence National Historical Park. **Page 8 (inset).** *The city of Philadelphia, as seen from the Jersey Shore* (1751). North Wind Picture Archives. **Page 11.** *The Bonhomme Richard V The Serapis, September 23, 1779*. By Thomas Butterworth (1768–1828). **Page 12.** *British prison ship* (c.1775). From Hulton Archives/Getty Images. **Page 15.** *A Day's Work: A Sampler of Historic Maine, Photographs 1860–1920, Part II*. From Gardiner, Maine, Tilbury House. **Page 16.** *Bending the Foresail*. Engravings by Darcy Lever (1819). From the Science, Industry and Business Division of the New York Public Library. **Page 19.** *The Art of Sailmaking as Practised in the Royal Navy by David Steel* (1807). From the Mariners' Museum.

Web Sites

Due to the changing nature of Internet links, PowerKids Press has developed an online list of Web sites related to the subject of this book. This site is updated regularly. Please use this link to access the list:
www.powerkidslinks.com/llwct/dlcsail/

www.ingramcontent.com/pod-product-compliance
Lightning Source LLC
Chambersburg PA
CBHW041121070526
44584CB00002B/235